What Do Software Engineers Do?

Careers in Computers

Rachael Morlock

COMPUTER SCIENCE For the REAL World™

Rosen Classroom™

Published in 2018 by The Rosen Publishing Group, Inc.
29 East 21st Street, New York, NY 10010

Book Design: Jennifer Ryder-Talbot
Editor: Caitie McAneney

Photo Credits: Cover goodluz/Shutterstock.com;p. 4-5 Dragon Images/ Shutterstock.com; p. 7 Georgejmclittle/Shutterstock.com; p. 8 Monkey Business Images/ Shutterstock.com; p. 11 michaeljung/Shutterstock.com; p. 12-13 nd3000/ Shutterstock.com; p. 15 Zakharchuk/Shutterstock.com; p. 16 science photo/ Shutterstock.com; p. 19 Herrndorff/Shutterstock.com; p. 20-21 ESB Professional/ Shutterstock.com.

Library of Congress Cataloging-in-Publication Data

Names: Morlock, Rachael.
Title: What do software engineers do?: careers in computers / Rachael Morlock.
Description: New York : Rosen Classroom, 2018. | Series: Computer Kids: Powered by Computational Thinking | Includes glossary and index.
Identifiers: LCCN ISBN 9781538353004 (pbk.) | ISBN 9781508162742 (library bound) | ISBN 9781508137979 (6 pack) | ISBN 9781538352656 (ebook)
Subjects: LCSH: Computer software--Development--Juvenile literature. | Computer programming--Vocational guidance--Juvenile literature.
Classification: LCC QA76.76.D47 M667 2018 | DDC 005.1--dc23

Manufactured in the United States of America

CPSIA Compliance Information: Batch #WS18RC: For Further Information contact Rosen Publishing, New York, New York at 1-800-237-9932

Table of Contents

The Age of Software

Software is a central part of our modern world. Without software, we wouldn't have websites, smartphones, video games, or email. The programs and systems that make computers and electronic devices work in a certain way are called software. Software works together with hardware, which is the collection of physical computer parts like screens, keyboards, computer chips, and printers. Every time you use a computer to search online, play a game, connect with friends, or write a paper, you use software that's been created just for those purposes.

Where does software come from? Software is **designed**, **developed**, **maintained**, tested, and **evaluated** by software engineers. A software engineer combines their knowledge of mathematics, computer science, and engineering to create useful computer programs.

Engineering is the process of creating and developing tools. To engineer software is to design and produce computer programs.

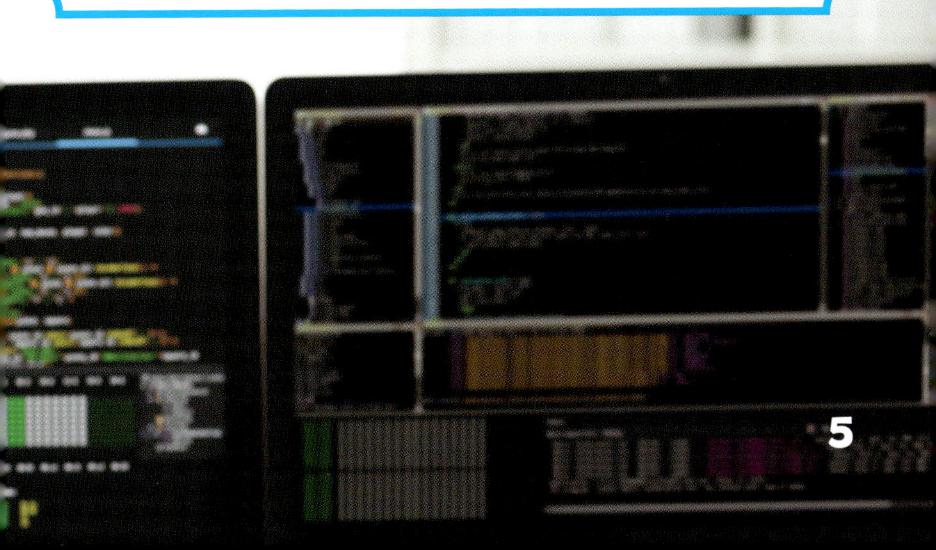

Computer Applications

Some software engineers are focused on computer applications, or **apps**. They work to understand the needs of future users of an app. When they have a clear idea of what software needs to do to be useful and productive, they can get to work designing and constructing it.

Even after software has been designed and built, the engineer's work is not finished. Many tests are performed to determine how well software functions and meets its goals. Software engineers are also responsible for maintaining software. If they've created a website or an app for a smartphone, they need to keep track of it to make sure it has updated information and that it continues to work smoothly.

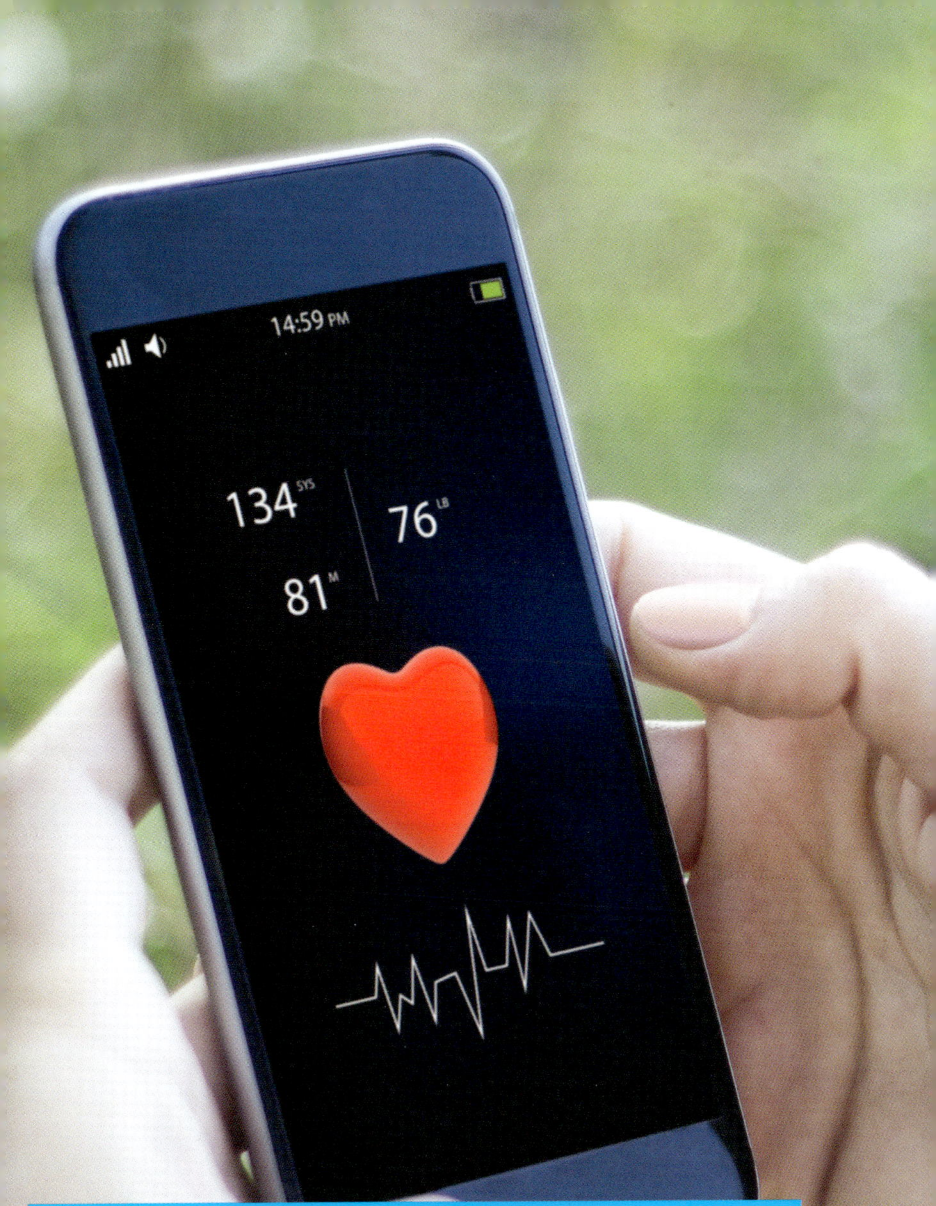

Software engineers develop many different kinds of apps. Their goal is to make software that's helpful and necessary, like a smartphone app that helps people keep track of their health.

maintain computer systems

install programs

improve systems

Systems Software Engineer

set up intranets

maintain security

give **technical support**

Systems software engineers pay attention to the goals and requirements of an organization. They can help install, or set up, the best software for an office.

Computer Systems

Sometimes software engineers focus their work on developing computer systems within their company or organization. Their job is to meet their group's needs for computer systems that are useful, secure, and connected. Systems software engineers often set up intranets, which are online networks that connect the computers and users within a certain organization.

Some software engineers work on computer systems outside of their own company. They consider and **research** the goals and needs of an organization. Then, they decide which systems and programs will be most helpful. These software engineers provide advice and technical support. By working to explain, set up, maintain, and repair systems, they make sure an organization has the software it needs to work well.

Where Do Software Engineers Work?

Software engineers play an important role in nearly every **industry**. Many of the places you visit, from the movie theater to the library, rely on computer software for their daily functions. Whether they provide services, manufacture parts, or sell goods, most organizations use software. As a result, software engineers are employed by businesses, schools, government agencies, and other organizations. Software engineering is growing in the fields of health care, green energy, car manufacturing, **aeronautics**, and all kinds of technology.

Since computers are their main tool, many software engineers work in an office setting. Some work in laboratories or research centers. Others work from their own homes. They can work for only one company or take on jobs from several different companies.

Software engineers can develop software that allows computers to test and control machinery.

Teamwork

Many software engineers work as part of a team. Team members perform different jobs based on the kind of organization they work for. In a large business, software engineers might work closely with hardware engineers, artistic designers, manufacturers, or salespeople. Together they take an idea and turn it into something that can be produced and sold.

Individuals might focus on just one part of software engineering, such as coding, when they work as a team.

On smaller projects, software engineers are sometimes responsible for completing all of the software engineering tasks by themselves. In other cases, they work together with other software engineers on large, in-depth projects. The tasks of designing, programming, testing, and evaluating software can be broken up among team members. Having input from multiple **experts** can make the creation of software smooth and efficient.

Programming

In order to develop programs and systems, software engineers must be able to use programming languages. Programming is the process of using detailed, orderly instructions to tell a computer what to do. A software engineer has to break down actions into simple steps a computer can follow. The set of instructions they create is called an algorithm. Once an algorithm is developed, it can be communicated to the computer using a programming language. The act of **translating** instructions into a programming language is known as coding.

Software engineers can choose from a variety of programming languages to find the best one for their software. Some of the most popular programming languages used by software engineers include C, C#, and Java.

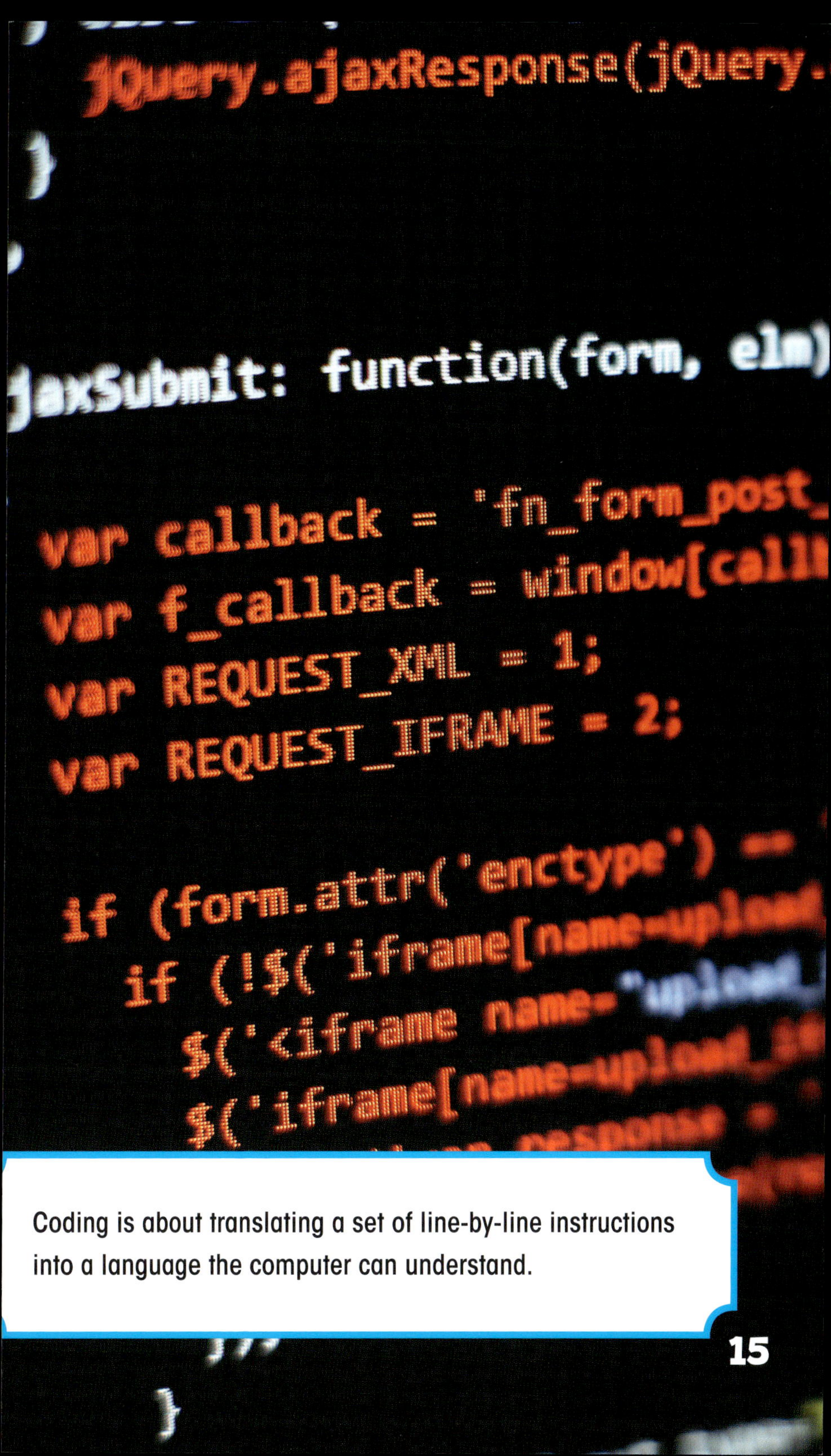

Coding is about translating a set of line-by-line instructions into a language the computer can understand.

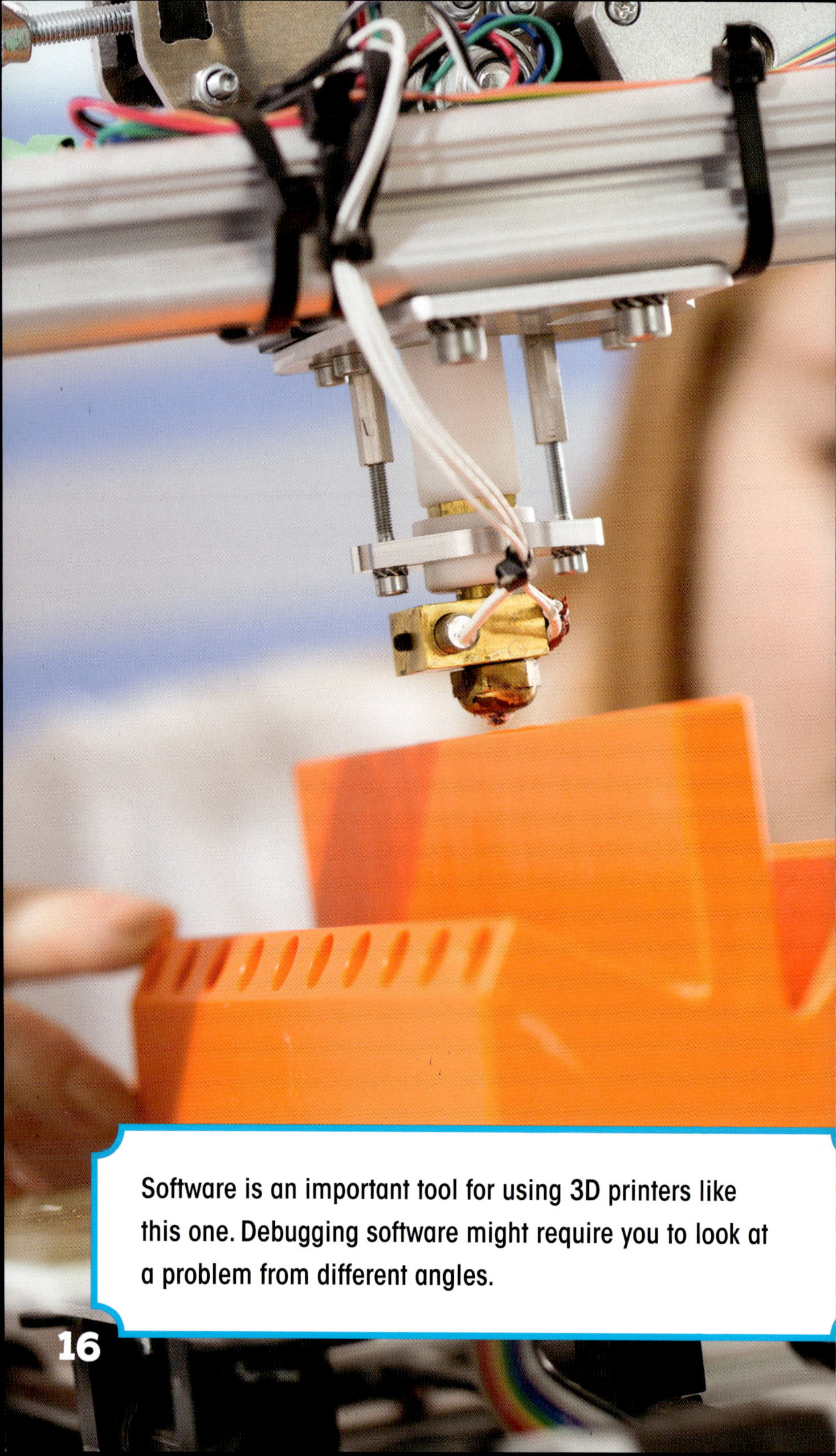

Software is an important tool for using 3D printers like this one. Debugging software might require you to look at a problem from different angles.

Persistence and Problem Solving

Designing software can be a challenging job. Software engineers use problem solving to work through the "bugs" in a program. In computer science, the act of identifying a problem, examining it, and finding a solution is called debugging. Mistakes and challenges are part of every creative process. The important thing is to take time to debug problems in order to create a working product.

Before software is finished, it must be carefully tested. Software is used in important and powerful ways. That means that software engineers have a big responsibility to make products that are dependable and free from mistakes. Testing a product helps a software engineer find and fix its weak spots. They have to be **persistent**, testing and retesting their software until it works.

Software Is Everywhere!

Think about an ordinary experience like going to the doctor. Usually, a nurse or doctor takes information about your height, weight, and temperature, then enters it into a computer. That computer uses software to keep track of information from each patient's visit. Software engineering is growing in the field of medicine. It can be used for creating databases, programming robots to assist with surgeries, and controlling devices used in health care.

As computers and mobile devices like smartphones become more commonplace, the possibilities for software engineers grow. Software is used by farmers checking their crops, pilots operating their planes, factories using robotic parts, mechanics fixing automobiles, and children using interactive websites. As new technology is developed, new software will be invented, too.

Software engineering is often used to develop assembly-line robots and computer-operated machines.

Becoming a Software Engineer

Software engineering is more popular than ever! With so many ways to use software, there are many openings for people who are talented enough to create it. However, there's more to software engineering than knowing how to use computers and devices, learn programming languages, and code. Software engineers also have to be good communicators, strong organizers, careful workers, and persistent problem solvers.

Many of the technical skills a software engineer needs can be learned at school. You can also start learning on your own through online programs, boot camps, and instruction books. Most working software engineers have earned college degrees in computer science or software engineering. Internships and jobs are also opportunities for new engineers to practice and learn skills.

There are many ways for kids to learn about computer science. Your school or local library might have classes or materials that can help you get started.

A Popular Job

In 2014, there were over a million software engineers working in the United States. That number is expected to increase as technology grows. It's not hard to see why software engineering is such a popular job! People who develop software have a chance to create something useful and positive that affects people all over the globe.

Every day, software engineers creatively find new and better ways of doing things. They are always learning about new technology, programming languages, and ways of improving the world around them. Since software is everywhere, software engineering can easily be combined with science, art, or any other subject. If you're interested in computers, problem solving, and making new things, the possibilities in software engineering are endless!

Glossary

aeronautics: A science dealing with the operation of aircraft.

app: A computer program that does a certain task.

design: To make the plan for how something should look or work.

develop: To create or produce through a process.

evaluate: To determine the condition of something.

expert: Someone with great knowledge about a certain subject.

industry: The businesses that provide a certain product or service.

maintain: To care for something by making repairs and changes when needed.

persistent: Continuing to do something despite challenges.

research: Studying to find something new.

technical support: Help with computer problems.

translate: To change from one language into another.

Index